Collective Security

T0346178

Collective Security

An Inaugural Lecture

by

ARNOLD D. MᶜNAIR, LL.D.

Whewell Professor of International Law:
Fellow of Gonville and Caius College

CAMBRIDGE

AT THE UNIVERSITY PRESS

1936

CAMBRIDGE
UNIVERSITY PRESS

University Printing House, Cambridge CB2 8BS, United Kingdom

Cambridge University Press is part of the University of Cambridge.

It furthers the University's mission by disseminating knowledge in the pursuit of
education, learning and research at the highest international levels of excellence.

www.cambridge.org
Information on this title: www.cambridge.org/9781316612774

© Cambridge University Press 1936

First published 1936
First paperback edition 2016

A catalogue record for this publication is available from the British Library

ISBN 978-1-316-61277-4 Paperback

COLLECTIVE SECURITY

Mr Vice-Chancellor, it would be a mistake to use this occasion for an attempt to say something which would be of interest only to my fellow international lawyers, and I prefer to try to answer some of the questions which are now stirring in the minds of many laymen as to the meaning of the term "Collective Security" and as to the true place of force in a system of international law. Two reasons impel me to do this. The first is that the Whewell Professor is particularly charged by the founder of his chair "to make it his aim in all parts of the subject to lay down such rules and to suggest such measures as may tend to diminish war and finally to extinguish war between nations". The second is that at present, unfortunately, we have in this University no chair of International Relations, so that the Whewell Professor may be forgiven if occasionally he strays a little across the frontier which divides law from politics, even when this can only be done at the cost of approaching the debatable zone of current controversy.

THE FORMER ATTITUDE
TOWARDS WAR

Let us put ourselves in the position of a student of international law in the first decade of this century who wanted to know what was the attitude of that system of law towards war. He would be told that three centuries ago Grotius, following some of his predecessors, had attempted to classify the causes of war (with particular reference to their bearing upon the attitude of third parties), and that, as Professor Brierly[1] has written, "at the heart of his system lay the attempt to distinguish between lawful and unlawful war" but that "this distinction never became part of actual international law" and "finally it disappeared even from

[1] *The Law of Nations*, pp. 25, 26.

theory". Our student would then turn to Hall's *International Law*, which was generally regarded as the most characteristically British exposition of the subject. There he would read that[1]

As international law is destitute of any judicial or administrative machinery, it leaves States, which think themselves aggrieved, and which have exhausted all peaceable methods of satisfaction, to exact redress for themselves by force. It thus recognizes war as a permitted mode of giving effect to its decisions.

Hall then points out that theoretically international law, professing to be a comprehensive system, "ought to determine the causes for which war can be justly undertaken", but has tried and found it impossible to do so. He adds that

it might also not unreasonably go on to discourage the commission of wrongs by investing a State seeking redress with special rights and by subjecting a wrong-doer to special disabilities,

[1] 5th ed. (1904), by J. B. Atlay, p. 60.

it would be idle for it to affect to impart the character of a penalty to war, when it is power-less to enforce its decisions. . . . International law has consequently no alternative but to accept war, independently of the justice of its origin, as a relation which the parties to it may set up if they choose, and to busy itself only in regulating the effects of the relation. Hence both parties to every war are regarded as being in an identical legal position, and consequently as being pos-sessed of equal rights.[1]

The Edwardian student would then turn to Westlake, of whom I like to remember that several of my colleagues were his col-leagues, and there he would read that[2]

International law did not institute war, which it found already existing, but regulates it with a view to its greater humanity. War is a piece of savage nature partially reclaimed, and fitted out for the purpose of such reclamation with legal effects, such as the abrogation or suspension

[1] *Ibid.* p. 61.
[2] *International Law*, vol. II, "War", 1st ed. 1907, 2nd ed. 1913, p. 3.

of treaties, and legal restrictions, such as what are called the laws of war and neutrality.

Westlake then adds[1] that

an attempt is sometimes made to determine in the name of international law the conditions on which a recourse may be had to arms...but these are not rules of law...and the legal character of a war is the same whether they have been observed or not. The truth is that when war enters on the scene all law that was previously concerned with the dispute retires, and a new law steps in, directed only to secure fair and not too inhuman fighting.

To the same effect writes Oppenheim, our much loved colleague by adoption:[2]

War is not inconsistent with, but a condition regulated by, International law. The latter at present cannot and does not object to States which are in conflict waging war upon each other instead of peaceably settling their difference.

Such were the opinions upon the relation of international law to war which I learned as a student. To regard the teachers whom

[1] *Ibid.* p. 4.
[2] *International Law*, vol. II. "War and Neutrality", 1st ed. 1906, 2nd ed. 1912, § 53.

I have quoted, as reactionaries would be absurd: they correctly described the contemporaneous attitude of international law towards war. Great efforts were made before and during that period, notably by the Conventions emanating from the two Hague Peace Conferences of 1899 and 1907, to introduce some order into the conduct of war, and those Conventions and the customary law underlying them had more success and effect than has been realized by laymen accustomed to see and hear more of their violation than of their normal operation. My immediate predecessor, Professor Pearce Higgins, made himself an acknowledged master of this branch of the law. His main inspiration, as I see it, was the desire to impress the public, and the generations of students here and naval officers at Greenwich who came under his influence, with a sense of the binding obligation of the rules which experience and humanity had evolved for placing some checks upon the licence and barbarity of war.

But there international law stopped. War itself was no illegality. Its outbreak might sometimes involve the breach of a treaty or some other international wrong, but it more frequently took rise in circumstances not falling within the sphere regulated by law. It was extra-legal rather than illegal. Whether or not the initiation of a war was a breach of law, the rules which regulated it, once it had broken out, were the same for both or all parties. And, what is more germane to my argument, the rules which governed the attitude of States not participating in a war towards the belligerents—the law of neutrality—were the same, regardless of the rights and wrongs of the war. A rigid impartiality in their conduct towards the belligerents was required by the law.

THE PRESENT ATTITUDE

All this changed some years ago—at any rate for the greater part of the world. Most international lawyers have realized that change for some time and have been expounding it, but the majority of laymen had not grasped the change until quite recently, and many of them are reluctant to admit the change even now. Let me mention three facts before I attempt to trace the development which has culminated in this change. Firstly, on October 9, 1935, war having broken out between two States, Italy and Abyssinia, fifty Governments, including our own, met in conference and put it on record that in their opinion Italy had "resorted to war in disregard of its Covenants under Article 12 of the Covenant of the League".

The second fact is that to-day fifty Governments are engaged in a series of measures, directed to handicap one of two belligerents in its contest with its adversary and eventually to make it impossible for it to continue the contest. Examine those measures, which are four in number: (1) an embargo on the export, re-export or transit to Italy and her possessions of arms, munitions and implements of war, while leaving their supply to Abyssinia unrestricted; (2) the prohibition of the grant of loans and credits to the Italian Government and all persons and corporations in Italian territory, while leaving the supply of similar facilities to Abyssinia unrestricted; (3) the prohibition of imports (other than gold and silver bullion and coin) from Italy into the co-operating countries, while leaving imports from Abyssinia unrestricted; (4) the prohibition of the export or re-export or transit to Italy and her possessions of a long list of "key materials", particularly minerals and transport animals, while leaving supplies to Abyssinia unrestricted.

The third fact is that our Government, which has always been foremost in pursuing a policy of strict impartiality in wars to which it is not a party, has recently passed a series of Orders in Council making it a penal offence for persons in the United Kingdom to carry on with one belligerent certain trades which in previous wars they have always been free to maintain with either or both belligerents so far as the law of this country is concerned.

Public opinion has been led up to these events so gradually and so patiently that their momentous character is obscured. I am not here concerned with British policy in regard to this dispute or with the questions whether sanctions might have been applied with greater determination and whether they ought to be increased. What I wish to emphasize is the legal character and the historical significance of what is now being done. The first feature is that it is an unheard of thing that fifty non-belligerents should meet and expressly concur in singling out one of two belligerents for condemnation as a treaty-breaker and an aggressor. The second is that most, if not all, of the measures now in force in the name of sanctions would twenty-five years ago have been serious breaches of the law of neutrality, affording to the victim of them good ground for reprisals or more serious action. There is no question but that these measures would have come as a surprise to Hall and Westlake[1] and above all to that exponent of the law of neutrality, Sir William Harcourt, the first Whewell Professor, had they not known of certain changes in the law which have intervened; for it is impossible to reconcile these measures with the duty of impartiality traditionally incumbent upon neutral States.

What then are these changes in the law and to what cause are they due? Let us deal with the second question first. The Great War of 1914 to 1918, by reason of the area affected by it, the destructive character of the instruments employed in it and the intensity of suffering on the part of combatants and non-combatants alike, produced a revulsion of feeling against war greater than that which usually follows the

[1] Westlake was fully alive to the moral necessity of the disappearance of the orthodox attitude of strict indifference: see his *Collected Papers*, pp. 375 *et seq.*

close of a war. Many were driven to hold the view, held by an increasing number to-day, that in no circumstances can the use of armed force as between States be justified and in no circumstances should it be resisted. Some base this view upon Christian or other principles of morality, and there are others who base it upon historical and personal experience, believing that no evil can be so great as the evils, spiritual and material, which flow from taking up arms or from resisting them, and that expressions such as "national self-defence" are merely phrases used by governments to delude their peoples. I have neither the skill nor the time to examine this view from any of these aspects, nor is it essential to my theme that I should do so; for this is not the view of force which was adopted by the Peace Conference of 1919.

THE POLICY OF COLLECTIVE
SECURITY

The treaties emanating from that Conference embody a new principle, commonly called the principle or policy of Collective Security, to which at present fifty-eight governments (including our own) stand pledged. Instead of the traditional legal indifference to the question of the responsibility for the outbreak of war there is substituted machinery for determining the party responsible and for condemning as illegal a resort to war without previously exhausting the machinery of the Covenant of the League for the settlement of disputes. In addition to the traditional right and duty of individual self-defence there is created a collective obligation to apply economic pressure in order to restrain an illegal resort to war, with an option to contribute armed force if necessary. On the one hand, war in breach of the Covenant is made illegal; on the other, force which is collectivized and placed at the service of the international community is made legal.

This new policy of collective security has suffered, I think, in popular esteem by being treated too much as a great ethical ideal and too little as a sound business proposition. It seems to me to rest on three main reasons. In the first place, experience of the old system has shown that the claim of one State to be so strong as to feel secure against a rival State involves, as has been repeatedly pointed out, a denial of a similar claim to the latter, with the result that it sets to work to tip the balance in its favour either by increasing its armaments or by concerting precarious alliances and ententes which in turn provoke counter-alliances and counter-ententes. Secondly, it is felt that if a State can count upon a substantial and reasonably adjacent portion of the international community coming to its aid, and, if necessary, pooling forces to protect it from aggression, it and likewise other States will be content with a lower level of armaments than if it has to rely only upon itself and any allies it can pick up and feel sure of. The third reason is that force is less likely to be abused if for the purely national and subjective test of the justification of a war there is substituted a collective judgment by parties other than the States involved and a collective condemnation of any war found by that external test to be illegal. This view was only imperfectly carried out by the Covenant, but, as we shall see, the Kellogg-Briand Pact to some extent remedies this deficiency. In a sentence, if so much can be compressed in a single sentence, the principle underlying the Covenant in relation to the preservation of peace is the creation of machinery for the settlement of disputes and for stigmatizing certain wars as illegal and the concerting of collective action against a State initiating an illegal war.

The machinery for the settlement of disputes takes two forms, firstly reference to the Permanent Court of International

Justice or a tribunal of arbitration, and secondly reference to the Council of the League for an attempt at conciliation and, failing that, for a Report which when adopted unanimously (excluding the disputing parties) has certain definite legal consequences, as has been illustrated by the dispute between Italy and Abyssinia. The first of these methods is voluntary except in so far as the parties have already bound themselves in advance, as for instance by what is called the "Optional Clause" of the Statute of the Permanent Court, to refer disputes of certain categories to judicial or arbitral settlement. The second is, for members of the League, obligatory; it is also residuary in character in that it sweeps up and governs disputes not settled by the first kind of machinery. The Permanent Court has, since it opened its doors in 1922, rendered more than sixty Judgments and Advisory Opinions, and in no instance has any party to the litigation defied the authority of the Court by refusing to give effect to its decision. I cannot digress into a discussion of the judicial and arbitral settlement of disputes beyond saying that the output of international law from judicial and arbitral sources since the World War has been prodigious. Coupled with the increase in multipartite treaties laying down rules of law, this output is rapidly transforming international law from a body of general principles resting mainly on text-book authority into a system of rules for which authority can be quoted from judicial and conventional sources, much in the same way as a modern system of national law rests on judgments and legislation. Forty-nine years ago Sir Henry Maine in a course of twelve Whewell Lectures[1] found it necessary to cite only two national judgments, one English and the other American, and one international award, the *Alabama*. A glance at a modern text-book of international law shows what an enormous ad-

[1] *International Law*, published by John Murray in 1894.

vance in the law-making process has been made in half a century.[1]

THE KELLOGG-BRIAND PACT

But the League machinery is limited in its scope. Only fifty-eight States and Dominions are bound by it and among the absentees are Germany, Japan and the United States of America. Outside the League there is frequent resort to judicial and arbitral machinery for the settlement of disputes, but there is no effective provision for collective action against an act of aggression upon a State not a member of the League; though in theory, but at present only in theory, the League machinery of collective action could be applied as between non-members.[2] Not only is member-

[1] The volumes of the *Annual Digest of Public International Law Cases* give a more eloquent testimony.

[2] If the League machinery succeeds in protecting Abyssinia against conquest by Italy, there is nothing to prevent it from being used, for instance, to protect Austria from being overrun by Germany.

ship of the League limited but the Covenant leaves outside its ban certain kinds of war, particularly war undertaken when the Council or the Assembly has announced its failure to reach a unanimous Report (excluding the disputing parties) and when three months have elapsed after that failure. Accordingly, in 1928 another change took place in the attitude of international society and international law towards war and is embodied in the Kellogg-Briand Pact, or Peace Pact of Paris as it is sometimes called. The articles of this simple document are two in number and are as follows:

Article 1

The High Contracting Parties solemnly declare in the names of their respective peoples that they condemn recourse to war for the solution of international controversies, and renounce it as an instrument of national policy in their relations with one another.

Article 2

The High Contracting Parties agree that the settlement or solution of all disputes or conflicts of whatever nature or of whatever origin they may be, which may arise among them, shall never be sought except by pacific means.

The distinctive characteristics of this Pact and its principal differences from the Covenant may be summarized as follows:

(*a*) the Pact has been accepted by sixty-two States and Dominions and is for all practical purposes universal in its territorial scope;

(*b*) the probable[1] effect of article two is to make any resort to armed force for the settlement of an international dispute illegal and thus avoids the technical point, prominent under the Covenant in the Sino-Japanese dispute of 1931 to 1933, that not every resort to armed force amounts to "war";

(*c*) it is a reasonable view, though I

[1] I say "probable" because there is some controversy on the question whether the words "except by pacific means" permit a resort to armed force which does not technically amount to war: see Lauterpacht in Oppenheim, *International Law*, vol. II (5th ed.), § 52 *l*.

cannot assert it to be an established opinion, that a breach of the Pact is a legal wrong not merely against the victim of the resort to armed force but also against the other signatories of the Pact;

(d) it contains *within it* no provision for collective sanctions, thus avoiding one of the main obstacles preventing the ratification of the Covenant of the League by the United States of America; but a breach of it can be met by its signatories, alone or collectively, by the measures[1] available for the prevention or redress of the breach of any other treaty, if they choose to take this course;

[1] What these measures may be is a highly controversial matter: see Lauterpacht in *Transactions of Grotius Society*, vol. xx (1935), pp. 178–202. It is worth noting that Mr Eden (as Minister for League of Nations Affairs) speaking in the House of Commons of a breach, not of the Kellogg-Briand Pact, but of the Covenant, said: "We do not consider that any Covenant-breaking State has any legal right to require the observance of other members of the League of any of the laws of neutrality." Hansard (Commons), vol. 305, p. 218 (October 23, 1935).

(*e*) most breaches of the Pact of 1928 will also be breaches of the Covenant, so that while the United States of America does not co-operate in the collective action under the Covenant the fact of their being a party to the Pact of 1928 tends to produce, between that country and the League, a coincidence in the condemnation of an aggressor, as happened in the recent Sino-Japanese dispute, and will, I hope, eventually happen in the case of the Italo-Abyssinian war.

Such then in the briefest outline are the two main documents which express in legal form the changing attitude of international society towards force. They may be summed up in two propositions: resort to armed force for the settlement of an international dispute is an illegal act, and, I submit, that illegal act is the commission of an international wrong (breach of treaty) against every State in the world (with unimportant exceptions such as Thibet) and not merely upon the victim of the use of force. That is the big new factor added by the Kellogg-Briand Pact. It is that which might, and, I think, would, justify a signatory of the Pact in conducting itself towards an aggressor in a manner which before the Pact would have amounted to unneutral conduct.

COLLECTIVE REVISION OF THE STATUS QUO

I have only touched on one aspect of the collective system—the collectivization of force. Equally important is the collective and peaceful revision of treaties and other international conditions whose continuance is a reasonable cause of friction. This principle is embodied in Article 19 of the Covenant and in Article 2 of the Pact of Rome made on the seventh of June, 1933, between France, Germany, Italy, and the United Kingdom, but in both cases only as a principle. There is urgent need of machinery to translate that principle into practice. It is also hinted at in Sir Samuel Hoare's speech to the League Assembly on September 11, 1935, when he referred to "fear of monopoly—of the withholding of essential colonial raw materials" and "the desire for a guarantee that the distribution of raw materials will not be unfairly impeded...". This is only a beginning. There are certain key commodities and key positions whose continuance in the sole control of a single Power or group of Powers produces a sense of unfairness and insecurity which will not be removed until that control (which is not the same as ownership) is vested in the hands of some international authority. I do not see how you can justify a situation in which one or a few Powers can hold others to ransom, if they choose to do so, because they happen to be in control of an international highway or a vital commodity.[1] If the control of such a highway

[1] For a summary of the distribution of minerals and mineral products including petroleum and the manner in which the denial of them to an aggressor

were international, the exercise of that control in aid of collective security would be easier to justify and to effect than it is while the control resides in national hands. There has been a good deal of talk recently of transferring colonies to Powers who have few or none and of the possession of a colonial empire as essential to the *amour propre* of a powerful nation. My own view is that to do anything which would tend to stereotype the colonial system in any of its present stages would be unfortunate. I regard them as transitional. I should prefer to see the colonial Powers encouraging (as we are doing) certain of their colonies to become self-governing communities. As for those colonies and protectorates not likely to be suited in the comparatively near future for this development, I consider that more would be gained than lost if many of them, though not all, were administered under

can be used as a collective sanction, see Sir Thomas H. Holland's most valuable book, *The Mineral Sanction* (1935).

some kind of international guardianship like the mandate system for the benefit of their inhabitants and the world at large. I may mention as features of that system the prohibition of native military forces for other than police purposes and local defence and the provision of the economic open door. All this lies outside the scope of this lecture. I merely remind my audience that a system which collectivizes the use of force and provides no machinery for the collective revision of the *status quo* is certain to fail, as has been cogently shown by Sir John Fischer Williams in his short book entitled *International Change and International Peace*. The direct and positive use of collective force for the revision of the *status quo* is in my opinion unthinkable. But it is worth considering whether as a first step consent to a revision may not be induced, indirectly and negatively, by making it clear that a State which obstinately declines to cooperate in a revision pronounced after due investigation to be essential to the general welfare cannot rely upon the use of collective force in support of an untenable claim.

THE ROLE OF THE INDIVIDUAL

I have mentioned only two great international instruments, the Covenant of the League and the Kellogg-Briand Pact, and I mention them because they are in force between fifty-eight and sixty-two States and Dominions respectively. But I could point to many other treaties drafted during the past seventeen years, some not in force, others only sparsely ratified, but all of them indications of the new movement on foot for the organization of collective action for the preservation of peace; for instance, the Draft Treaty of Mutual Assistance of 1923, the "Geneva Protocol" of 1924, the "General Act of Arbitration" of 1928, the Convention of Financial Assistance of 1930, the Convention to Improve the Means of Preventing War of 1931, the Rio de Janeiro Pact of Non-Aggression and Conciliation of 1933, *et cetera*. In view of this persistent effort is it possible for any fair-minded man to dismiss this movement by saying that a zealous band of visionaries in 1919 stampeded the Allied Powers into the adoption of a crazy scheme? Is it not a more reasonable interpretation to regard these developments as evidence, in General Smut's memorable phrase, that "mankind is on the march" and seeking for some new form of organization in which we can retain and develop our national life and characteristics without the constant fear and frequent happening of the collisions between national groups which throw back civilization and now threaten to overwhelm it? At any rate I submit to you the view that this is the correct interpretation of the years since the Armistice of November 1918. I also suggest that it is primarily to the individual citizen that we must look to supply the driving force behind this movement and not to his government. It has been accepted as the business of governments to promote the interests of the nations whose professional champions they are. It is inevitable that governments should be reluctant to abate one iota of their clients' interests, and it is only when they can be absolutely convinced that in the long run the interests of the international community coincide with those entrusted to them that most of them will move a step in an international direction. Some of them are very hard to convince. The application of collective security involves risks; but the success of flagrant aggression in breach of solemn treaties is a danger to avert which some risk is justified, and the risk will diminish as the precedents for successful collective action accumulate.

Most great movements in public affairs originate with individuals, not with governments. It was a popular movement in this countrywhichcompelledourrepresentatives at Vienna in 1815 to insist upon annexing to the Congress Treaty a condemnation of the slave trade and later made the British Government the protagonist in the suppression of that evil. It was the devotion of a single Swiss citizen, Dunant, which infected a group of his fellow-countrymen with his zeal and ultimately induced his government to convoke a conference and secure the adoption of the Geneva Red Cross Convention of 1864. The League of Nations originated in the parallel work of two groups of citizens, one in our country and the other in the United States of America. It is, I submit, only by the action of individuals—in those countries in which the individual is still allowed to develop and express opinions—in maintaining a constant pressure upon their governments that this new movement can be brought to fruition.

THE LEAGUE AND ARMED FORCE

What is happening now is not that force is being abolished. It is being collectivized, denationalized. The manner of its exercise remains national: the judgment which precedes and authorizes its exercise is collective.[1] When thus authorized, it acquires the character of a public sanction, while its actual exercise remains in private hands. Such, as I see it, is the essence of the system of collective security towards which the world, or at any rate Europe in the first place, is groping its way and which is at the moment on trial. Hitherto there has

[1] There is at present a movement for the creation of an *international* force, that is, a force recruited by and responsible to a truly international organ. I do not propose to state here why I think that this proposal is not at present within the field of practical politics. I will merely point out that such a force is something quite different from *collective* force contributed by States in support of the policy of collective security. Among other differences there is the fact that in the case of collective force the responsibility for its use rests with governments, whereas the decision to use an international force would presumably rest with the individuals in control of the international organ. There are many who will prefer that a decision to employ armed force ought only to be taken by governments; for they are likely to realize that in so doing they are staking the future of their countries, and will probably act with a greater sense of responsibility than a group of individuals, though, it must be admitted, often with less promptitude.

been a tendency to assume that it is the League whose duty it is to afford security, but we are now beginning to realize that it is upon the League's members that this duty rests. If we think that the principle of collective security can be established without incurring risk, we delude ourselves. To say, as some are now saying, that the Covenant does not contemplate the possible necessity of the use of armed force as part of that collective action is completely erroneous. It is only necessary to read Articles 10 and 16 of the Covenant and the British official "Commentary" on the Covenant published in 1919, while the memorandum addressed to the League Committee on Arbitration and Security in 1928 by the United Kingdom Government[1] and many other official declarations are to the same effect. Moreover, we have constantly been told that it is necessary to maintain our armaments at a level adequate

[1] League of Nations Official Journal, May 1928, p. 694.

to enable us to carry out our obligations under the Covenant, and as recently as December 21, 1935, the Chancellor of the Exchequer is reported in *The Times* to have said that it would be "the duty of the Government in these coming years to restore our defence forces to a level at which we can feel that not only have we secured the safety of this country and those great trade routes between us and the other members of the British Empire upon which our existence depends, *but we are also in a position to back up our collective action at the League....*"[1] No member of the League is compelled to contribute armed force in defence of the Covenant, but in certain events the Covenant authorizes it to do so if in its discretion it should think fit. Moreover, a member of the League before co-operating in any sanction that is likely to provoke an attack by the aggressor affected by it must realize that in such an event it will be necessary to use force. It has therefore a right to

[1] Italics mine.

receive in advance from a reasonably powerful section of its co-operators specific and satisfactory assurances of the mutual support stipulated for by paragraph three of Article 16.

UNITED STATES OF AMERICA

As for the United States of America, I will only say this. No reasonable person, in the present position of international affairs, can count upon that country contributing armed force for the repression of an aggressor in pursuance of a system of collective security. But is it too much to expect that when there is a clear breach of the Kellogg-Briand Pact and in consequence a breach of a treaty with that country, the American Government, which with France was primarily responsible for the Pact, should reply to the breach of treaty by departing from the traditional law of neutrality and preventing its citizens from frustrating the efforts of its fellow-signatories of that Pact by trading with a proclaimed aggressor? In the present Italo-Abyssinian dispute the President has[1] "warned American citizens against transactions of any character with either of the belligerent nations except at their own risk". This warning does not in terms discriminate between the aggressor and the victim of the aggression. But if it means that the American Government would refrain from protecting American trade with the aggressor from interception by a group of States applying sanctions, then indirectly the new American policy would work in favour of collective security.

CONCLUSION

When I consider our own place in this movement, I sometimes think of Watts' picture entitled "For he had Great Possessions". We too have done pretty well out of the old system. Are we going to turn our back like the man in that picture on this new move-

[1] *Bulletin of International News*, Nov. 9, 1935, p. 60.

ment or are we going to shoulder our share of the responsibility and play our part with all the risks which the new policy entails? It is difficult for us at home to realize how much other countries look to us to give the lead in this matter which our position entitles them to expect. I do not think I am guilty of national presumption when I say that our attitude towards the movement is one of outstanding and perhaps decisive importance. In the past two years the two periods during which our national prestige in the world has been at its highest have been those during which we have been taking a lead in the use of collective action in the interests of peace. The first period was when we proposed at Geneva that a collective force should be admitted to the Saar Territory and be responsible to the Governing Commission of that Territory for the maintenance of order during the danger-ous time of the plebiscite and before the handing back of the Territory to Germany. That force was contributed by Italy, Holland, Sweden and ourselves. The second was the period represented by Sir Samuel Hoare's great speech in the League Assembly on September 11th, 1935, reaffirming his country's support of the League's obligations "for the collective maintenance of the Covenant in its entirety and particularly for steady, collective resistance to all acts of unprovoked aggression", and by our subsequent leadership in the policy of sanctions. During both these periods our international standing has been pre-eminent. During both our Government has commanded a more united national support than democratic Governments usually enjoy. But, as Sir Samuel Hoare said, "if the burden is to be borne it must be borne collectively". We cannot do more than our fair share. If through other nations failing to do their share the movement towards collective security receives a check, it must be no more than a check. We must make it clear that only those who are prepared to share the burden can expect to enjoy the benefit. *Qui sentit commodum sentire debet et onus.* But if we are patient and hold firm to our declared policy, which comprises collective revision as well as collective security, my belief is that eventually the principle of collective security will be established, that, though at first limited in territorial scope, it will spread, and that it will introduce a new and saner epoch in international relations, an achievement in which we shall not be sorry to have taken a leading part.